THE RAILROADS
OPENING THE WEST

OPENING THE WEST
THE RAILROADS
DENNIS R. FLATLEY

Franklin Watts
New York / London / Toronto / Sydney
A First Book/1989

Cover photograph courtesy of The Granger Collection

Photographs courtesy of:
The Granger Collection: pp. 8, 10, 11, 13, 14, 24–25, 27,
30–31, 45, 50, 53, 57, 59 (top and bottom); Association
of American Railroads: pp. 19, 23, 29, 39; Sheldon Pen-
noyer: p. 21; Baltimore & Ohio Railroad: p. 33; New
York Public Library Picture Collection: p. 51.

Library of Congress Cataloging in Publication Data

Flatley, Dennis R.
The railroads: opening the West/Dennis R. Flatley.
p.   cm. — (A First book)
Bibliography: p.
Includes index.
Summary: Discusses the building and development of railroads in
the United States from 1800 to the Civil War and the effect this
had on the nation.
ISBN 0-531-10682-9
1. Railroads — United States — History — 19th century — Juvenile
literature. [1. Railroads — United States — History — 19th century.]
I. Title. II. Series.
HE2751.F59 1989
385'.0973 — dc19
88-30335   CIP   AC

CONTENTS

For my wife
and all
my grandchildren

THE RAILROADS
OPENING THE WEST

Traveling through the wilderness
of seventeenth-century America on foot,
on horseback, and by sedan chair

1 EARLY TRANSPORTATION IN AMERICA

This is the era of airliners and spacecraft. Boys and girls look forward to space travel and plan to be astronauts, scientists, and engineers. A century and a half ago another kind of "engineer" interested youngsters. These were the railroad engineers who drove the engines, or locomotives, of their time. Those early locomotives could transport freight and passengers at 15 to 40 miles (24 to 64 km) per hour, amazing speeds for their day. We have almost forgotten the long-haul railroads and their contributions to business, science, engineering, and the exploration of the United States.

Until the early 1800s, travel was on foot, on horseback, or by boat. Freight was moved by ocean-going ships and riverboats. Since roads were primitive, animal-drawn wagons were used only for short distances in and around towns and settle-

The establishment of an eighteenth-century American farm site

ments. As the people spread westward from the East Coast, a road would be built from one farm or settlement to the next one further inland.

Passenger Travel / The first regularly scheduled stagecoach run between New York and Philadelphia was started in 1756. The stagecoach was a large closed coach usually pulled by a team of four horses. It took a coach traveler three days to cover the 90 miles (145 km) between the two cities. By

An accident on an early road. Primitive roads meant
that surfaces could be knee-deep in dust, mud, or snow.

1811, there were four stage lines between New York and Philadelphia that ran on a regular basis. The fastest coach line was called the Express, cost $8.00 for a one-way fare, and covered the distance between the two cities in about twelve hours. The slowest of the four lines was named Diligence, and it took twenty-six hours to travel the 90 miles.

Sending Freight / To send freight by wagon over those same 90 miles (145 km) took three days in 1756; it had improved only slightly by the early 1800s. Freighting by wagon was as expensive as it was slow. The list of items sent by wagon was very small. Only things that could not be produced locally, such as tea, iron, salt, and gunpowder, would be sent by wagon. Often the freight charges cost as much as or more than the item had cost to buy.

In 1810, a farmer in far-western New York state could grow wheat that was worth 50 cents a bushel. To ship that same bushel of grain to New York City would cost him at least half that amount, or 25 cents a bushel.

Even worse, a farmer around Pittsburgh, Pennsylvania (379 miles, or 610 km, from New York City) had to ship his produce 1,200 miles (1,900 km) down the Ohio and Mississippi rivers to New Orleans, where it would be loaded on ships and sent

*In early America, flatboats were
used to transport goods.*

to the East Coast port cities. This was very costly, because the round trip took three months. The trip was also dangerous because a whole year's crop could be lost in a storm or threatened by river pirates.

In 1807, the success of Robert Fulton's steamboat, the *Clermont*, set the pace for the next twenty years' development of the inland waterways, mak-

Robert Fulton's steamboat, the Clermont

ing them the nation's major source of passenger and freight transportation. In 1800, passage from Pittsburgh to New Orleans had cost $60.00 per person and $6.75 per ton of freight. By 1820 the regular navigation of the Ohio and Mississippi rivers by steamboats reduced these costs by half. The increased number of riverboats and the lower costs helped to settle the lands along the bigger rivers. However, the problem of settling land away from the rivers remained. Goods could be moved by river from New Orleans to Louisville, Kentucky, for what it cost to send them by wagon to an Indiana farmer who lived only 20 miles (32 km) north of that river city.

Along the East Coast, the overland transportation problem was as great. Easterners paid $9.00 to bring a ton of freight the 3,000 miles (5,000 km) by sea from Europe. That same $9.00 would move that ton of freight only 30 miles (48 km) inland by wagon.

Setting the Stage / In the early stages of settling the United States, even the poor roads and riverboats worked well enough to bring people to the new territories. But the nation needed better transportation if it was to continue to grow. The stage was set for the opening of the West by the railroads!

THE GROWTH OF THE RAILROADS

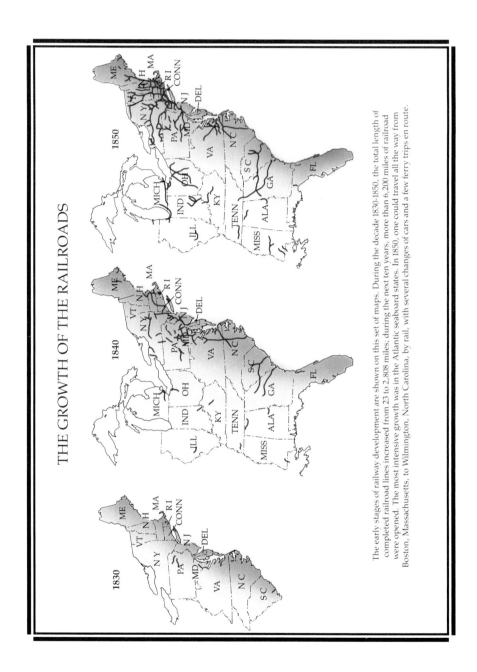

The early stages of railway development are shown on this set of maps. During the decade 1830-1850, the total length of completed railroad lines increased from 23 to 2,808 miles; during the next ten years, more than 6,200 miles of railroad were opened. The most intensive growth was in the Atlantic seaboard states. In 1850, one could travel all the way from Boston, Massachusetts, to Wilmington, North Carolina, by rail, with several changes of cars and a few ferry trips en route.

2 BEGINNING THE RAILROADS

The first railroads ran not with steam, but with animal power. Four hundred years ago railroads were used in Germany and in the English coalfields near Newcastle. All of these early railways used wooden rails and flanged wooden wheels, but the wooden surfaces caused slipping when they were wet and wore out quickly. Soon cast-iron wheels were being tried in place of wooden ones, but they destroyed the wooden rails even more quickly than the wooden wheels did. The solution was all-cast-iron rails.

Railroads Come to America / By 1800, the first American railway was in use. It was a short gravity railroad with wooden rails for tracks. The cars ran down a hill because of their own weight, and were pulled back up the hill by animal power or cable. Short railroads using horses or mules were built in Massachusetts, Pennsylvania, Virginia, and New

Hampshire and moved heavy freight such as bricks, coal, and quarried stone for short distances.

The Granite Railway was the first of the American railways built before 1825. It moved the granite used to build the Bunker Hill Monument, in Boston.

The second railway built was the Mauch Chunk Switch-Back Railway in Mauch Chunk, Pennsylvania. It moved coal from the Lehigh mine fields to the Lehigh River.

The Pioneer Steam Enthusiasts / Oliver Evans, a Philadelphia inventor, built in 1804 the first steam-powered vehicle to move on the roads of the new nation. His Oruktor Amphibilos was basically a riverboat, a combination *steam dredge* and paddle-wheel barge. The vehicle was mounted on four cart wheels, making it the first self-propelled amphibious craft in the world.

Evans predicted in 1812 that "The time will come when carriages propelled by steam will be in general use . . ." Although his predictions were to come true in just twenty-five years, Evans was considered "daft" by many of the people of his time.

Colonel John Stevens on October 23, 1824, became the first man to run a steam-powered locomotive on rails in the Americas. His "Steam Wagon" made 12 miles (19 km) per hour on his estate in Hoboken, New Jersey, on a circular 220-foot (67-m) cog track, or *rack-rail track*, carrying six house guests as passengers. However, Stevens's locomotive was just experimental and was never used commercially.

The first steam engine in America to carry passengers was the "rack rail," designed by Colonel John Stevens. It was used for demonstration purposes only.

Some of Stevens's backers continued to work for the cause of railroading by forming an organization called the Society for Internal Improvement. The group started and supported an educational campaign to show the public that railroads were as useful as canals for transportation purposes. Four years later, in 1828, the Pennsylvania Board of Canal Commissioners voted for a combination system involving both canals and railways. In March of that year, the state set aside $2 million to build the Philadelphia and Columbia Railroad.

The next advance in American railroading was provided by the chief engineer of a canal company, John Bloomfield Jervis. Jervis imported two locomotives from England, the *America* and the *Stourbridge Lion*.

The *Stourbridge Lion* was the first steam locomotive to run on a commercial line in the Americas. Jervis constructed a set of tracks especially for the *Lion*'s test run. The rails were made of hemlock wood. A 32-foot-high (10 m) wooden trestle or bridge, a single curve, and a 2½-mile (4 km) straightaway made up the test run.

It was a successful test run without incident, but the *Lion*'s first run was its only one. It was too heavy for practical use and was converted to a stationary engine to drive machinery.

The Stourbridge Lion

Beginning the New Railroads / By 1810, Baltimore had become the third largest city in the United States. Because of its port and its famous *clipper ships*, Baltimore became the fastest growing of our export trading centers. In the next ten years its population almost doubled, from 35,300 in 1810 to 62,700 in 1820. By the late 1820s, though, Baltimore was facing a problem: the Erie Canal was giving New York City the advantage over Baltimore in doing business with the Western settlements. Baltimore's worried business and municipal leaders looked to the new railroad industry to help their city continue its growth. At their request, the state of Maryland granted a charter to the Baltimore and Ohio Railroad Company on February 28, 1827. The new company moved quickly to become the first American public railroad with regularly scheduled service.

Sixteen months after receiving its charter, the B&O started construction on July 4, 1828. The last living signer of the Declaration of Independence, ninety-one-year-old Charles Carroll, laid the railroad's first foundation stone. He said, "I consider this among the most important acts in my life, second only to my signing the Declaration of Independence. If even it be second to that." By January 7, 1830, the B&O had established regularly scheduled service between Baltimore and Ellicott's Mills, 14

The first "trains" on the Baltimore & Ohio
Railroad were drawn by horses.

miles (22.5 km) to the west. However, this service was horse-drawn, not steam-powered.

The first regularly scheduled steam-powered service on a public railroad was provided by a much less well-known railway, the South Carolina Canal and Railroad Company. While never as famous as the B&O, the SCC&R gained an important place in railroad history because of its choice for its chief engineer, Horatio Allen.

When Allen left his position as assistant to John Jervis at the Delaware and Hudson Canal Company, he brought with him a strong interest in steam-powered locomotives. Allen fought an uphill battle with the board of directors of the SCC&R to convince them to use steam power on the new railroad. Before they agreed to use steam, they had experimented with wind power (using sail cars) and a horse-powered treadmill (using a horse walking on an endless belt to drive the wheels).

The Best Friend of Charleston,
the first locomotive built in the
United States for regular service

Horatio Allen was eventually successful, and a steam locomotive was ordered, built, and named the *Best Friend of Charleston*. On December 25, 1830, the *Best Friend* became the first American-built locomotive placed in regular service. It pulled two wooden wagons loaded with passengers from Charleston to the end of the line, at State and Dorchester roads. This first run ushered in the future—regularly scheduled steam-powered public railroad service.

3 EARLY EXPANSION

In January 1831, there were only 32 miles (51.5 km) of railroad tracks in use in the United States. But businessmen and bankers had already discovered its worth.

In the Southeastern states—Virginia, the Carolinas, and Georgia—the need for railroads was tied to the South's major crop, cotton, which was grown on huge farms called plantations.

The riverboats carried the cotton grown on the flatlands along the rivers to river ports like Savannah and New Orleans. From there the cotton was sent by ship to the factories of the North. Landlocked cotton-growing areas needed rail transportation to allow them to compete with those cotton growers served by the riverboat system. Railroads could transport cotton grown on the isolated inland plains and the eastern foothills of the Alleghenies directly to ports. From there it was shipped to Northern factories.

In the North, the Erie Canal was giving New York State, especially New York City, a great advantage in trading with the Midwest. In this wealthy trade, the Midwest received much-needed goods produced in the East and Europe and the fast-growing population of the East Coast received Midwestern crops.

*A lock on the Erie Canal
at Lockport, New York*

Maryland and the states to the north backed railroads to keep their port cities thriving. Already the largest port, New York seemed about to become the only one still expanding.

The Tom Thumb *Experiment* / The Baltimore & Ohio (B&O) has been in continuous operation since 1830. It is the oldest railroad in existence in the United States.

On its first regularly scheduled public service, it used horses to pull its railroad cars. But it was not long before the B&O would begin to experiment with steam, thanks to the efforts of Peter Cooper.

Cooper was a land investor who had bought 3,000 acres of land along the Baltimore and Ohio's *right-of-way* in the hope of a large profit once the railroad was built. When the company's directors were slow in building the railroad, Cooper built his own steam locomotive, the *Tom Thumb*. As its name suggests, it was a small locomotive. Its one cylinder produced only 1.43 *horsepower*, compared to the modern diesel locomotive's 1,500 to 3,000 horse-power. But the *Tom Thumb* was small even for its own time—so small, in fact, that many people considered it to be no more than a toy or a model.

Yet despite its size, in August 1830 the *Tom Thumb* became the first American-built locomotive

The Tom Thumb

to run on a public railroad in the United States. It was the B&O's first experiment with steam and marked the turning point in the company's history.

On that August day, Cooper drove the *Tom Thumb*, which pulled an open car carrying eighteen passengers. During the second half of the run, a famous race took place between the locomotive and a horse-drawn B&O railroad car. The

The race between the B & O's Tom Thumb *and a horse-drawn car*

story has it that the *Tom Thumb* was ahead when a blower fan belt failed, forcing Cooper to slow down and allowing the horse-drawn car to win the race. When it was over, the victorious B&O horsemen had a laugh at the expense of the upstart little locomotive and its builder-engineer.

But the joke was really on them; it was the *Tom Thumb* and Cooper who came off with the final victory. The locomotive had averaged 9⅓ miles (15 km) per hour on that first run in spite of its size and the fan-belt problem. The B&O directors were now impressed with the possibilities of steam-powered locomotives. They no longer considered the *Tom Thumb* a toy, and now agreed with Cooper that steam was the way to go.

Improvements in Track / The new, heavy steam locomotives could pull heavier loads than horses could, and pull them faster. But the locomotives seemed to create as many problems as they solved.

The rails at that time were made of wood covered with strap iron, and were far too weak to take the heavy pounding of steam locomotives. Eventually, the iron straps on top of the rails would work loose from the supporting rail, and sometimes the end of the strap would curl upward, forming what was called a "snakehead."

A snakehead was a double threat. First, it could derail a moving train; that is, cause it to jump off the track. Derailments can injure or kill passengers and crew, and damage equipment and freight. Second, a snakehead could suddenly smash through the floor of a moving car, frightening, injuring, or even killing passengers.

The snakehead problem was solved in 1830 by Robert Stevens, the president and engineer for the Camden and Amboy Railroad in New Jersey. Stevens, the son of Colonel John Stevens (see Chapter Two), designed a kind of all-cast-iron rail, called

Among the different types of railroad track used by America's pioneer railroad builders was one made up of wooden stringers with iron straps laid on top.

the T rail. The use of a solid-iron rail was not new in itself (see Chapter Two). What was unique about this rail, however, was its shape. In cross section, the T rail resembles the capital letter T.

Stevens designed the T rail while sailing to England to buy a locomotive and rails for the Camden and Amboy. During the voyage, he carved out a wooden cross section of the T rail, to provide a model for the English foundries that would make the cast-iron rails.

His new rail design was first used by Stevens's own Camden and Amboy Railroad, and later adopted by engineers of the B&O. Eventually, the T rail became the standard rail design for the world's railroads. Today T rails are made of machine-forged steel instead of cast iron.

Robert Stevens also solved—this time accidentally—another major problem of early railroads. In those days, railroads used blocks of stone, called *sills*, to support the rails. The blocks were laid in parallel lines along the *roadbed*. But sills would break, sink, or allow the rails to pull loose. If such damaged track was not discovered and repaired, it could cause dangerous derailments.

When the quarry digging the stone for the Camden and Amboy could not meet the delivery schedule, Stevens was faced with a problem. The locomotive he had ordered was due to arrive. He had the required rails for the track, but needed the sills to support them. Stone was in short supply for the moment, but there was plenty of wood available, so Stevens decided to use wood ties temporarily to support the rails. He had the ties laid crosswise (at a 90-degree angle) to the rails and under them.

Probably no one, including Stevens, expected the wooden ties, called crossties, to be used for very long. But surprisingly, the crossties proved to be strong and flexible enough to take the pounding of a heavy locomotive. They were much better all around than stone sills.

That "temporary" change that Stevens made proved permanent, along with his other track improvement, the all-metal T rail. His combination of T rail and wood crosstie remains the worldwide standard for railroad track.

Boston and the Railroads / The New England railroads got a somewhat later start than the South Carolina Canal and Railroad Company and the Baltimore and Ohio. A few business leaders in New England who were interested in the railroads, in 1827, arranged for Boston to be the site of the first railroad exposition in America. Three years later, the Boston and Lowell Railroad (the parent company of the current Boston and Maine Railroad) was chartered. It was followed by the Boston and Worcester and the Boston and Providence railroads in 1831.

The Boston and Worcester Railroad (parent company of the Boston and Albany Railroad) was the first to get into service. It opened a 7-mile (11-

km) stretch between Boston and Newton and began regular passenger service on April 16, 1834. Worcester, which was 44 miles (71 km) from Boston, was reached in July 1835, but Springfield, which was only 53 miles (85 km) beyond Worcester, was not opened until March 1839.

Other Developments / In 1836, an idea for an improved type of wagon toll road was brought from Toronto, Canada, to western New York State. It was a "plank road" and helped to open the West. The roads were constructed in the following way. Two parallel rows of "small timbers" were embedded in the ground about the same distance apart as the rails in railroad track (about 4 feet or 1.2 m). On top of these "stringers," as they were called, planks were placed at right angles to the road's direction. These "plank roads" provided a very satisfactory all-weather wagon road. Their building cost, $1,000 to $2,400 per mile, was very small, considering railroads could and did cost thirty times that amount per mile.

These plank roads, often nicknamed "farmer's railroads," allowed goods and produce to be moved at a lower cost. A horse could haul almost three times as much weight as it could on other types of roads (due to greatly reduced friction between the wagon wheels and the road's surface). The all-weather surface also allowed the farmer to transport his produce and goods when he couldn't do other work, such as during wet or winter weather. Since a farmer could get more to market more quickly and without interrupting his other work, he could charge less for his crops and still make a higher profit.

Plank roads quickly spread throughout the Midwest and South, from Michigan to Alabama. Whether they were built in direct competition with railroads or as farm-to-market roads to bring goods to and from the railroads, they helped to open the West.

As the 1830s came to a close, the total railroad track mileage had grown to 2,808 miles (4,519 km), the number of railroads had grown to 409, and 19 states had railroads. From New England to Georgia, the railroads of the United States were ready to cross the Appalachians and connect the East Coast with the other side of that great mountain range.

4 CONQUERING THE MOUNTAINS

In the 1840s the railroads would prove themselves a better means of transportation than the canals and roads. The most important challenge would be connecting the East Coast with the Midwest—the great Mississippi-Missouri-Ohio river basin.

Winning Support / The enemies of the railroads often played on people's fears in their publicity campaigns. For example, as late as 1839, the canal, turnpike, and stagecoach companies and their investors were using posters to frighten the citizens of Philadelphia. The campaign was an attempt to stop construction on the Camden and Amboy Railroad. One such poster warned mothers about the safety of "YOUR LITTLE ONES," using such phrases as "must you be hurried home to mourn a DREADFUL CASUALTY!" The poster used a drawing of a train striking a horse and carriage while a woman runs in fear and a man asks a policeman for help. The text

*A poster intended to stir up opposition to
the further construction of railroads*

of the poster warned citizens of "the RUIN of your TRADE" and "annihilation [complete destruction] of your RIGHTS." It asked if they would "consent to be a SUBURB OF NEW YORK!!" and ended by pleading, "RALLY PEOPLE in the Majesty of your Strength and forbid THIS OUTRAGE!"

This type of poor publicity, added to the financial failure of many railroads, made it difficult for the new industry. Even so, the early railroaders solved many of their mechanical and construction problems. They not only survived, but they competed successfully with the canals. By 1840, the railroads came within 500 miles (800 km) of equaling the canals in the number of miles constructed (2,808 vs. 3,300 miles, or 4,519 vs. 5,311 km). This was done for less than one-third of the cost of the canals. Although the canals could move freight at a lower cost than the railroads could, all of the Northern canals were closed three to five months each year because of either ice or a water level that was too high or too low. The railroad's greater speed and ability to deliver year-round impressed businessmen and investors. While the Erie and a few other canals would continue to make money for many years, even gaining more business through the 1850s, their mileage would stop expanding at 3,700 (6,000 km) during the 1840s. The railroads would move on to reach 9,000 miles (14,500 km), more than tripling their track mileage at the start of the 1840s.

Five Make the Challenge / The Appalachian Mountains are the coastal mountains of the eastern United States, a series of overlapping ranges running from Maine to Alabama. Five railroads (the Boston and Albany, the New York Central, the Erie, the Pennsylvania, and the Baltimore and Ohio) were to challenge the Appalachians during the 1840s.

Boston to Albany / In 1833, the Boston and Worcester Railroad received a second charter for the Western Railroad Corporation. This line would be the second leg of the Boston-to-Albany connection. It would run from Worcester through Springfield to the New York State border, about 30 miles (48 km) short of the final goal, Albany.

On October 1, 1839, the 55-mile (89 km) section between Worcester and Springfield opened. Soon the road was operating daily service with two trains in each direction. In 1840, the Western obtained permission to build the Albany and West Stockbridge Railroad as the final leg of the Boston-to-Albany route. While the A&WS was under construction, the Western leased the use of the Hudson and Berkshire Railroad. The H&B would be used for a two-year period after the completion of the other sections of the Boston-to-Albany route. This plan allowed for an early completion of at least a temporary route that would open the Boston-to-Albany connection.

Its opening was marked by a three-day celebration that began on December 27, 1841, starting in Albany and ending in Boston. By May 1842, the line was sending forty to sixty cars of freight traveling both east and west each day. The first of the port cities had opened a rail route through the Appalachians to the West!

The Other Four / The Erie moved slowly across the southern part of New York. Bothered by financial problems, bad management, and poor construction, it would not be completed until April 1851, almost ten years after the Boston-to-Albany route opened.

The next route to be opened belonged to the Pennsylvania Railroad, although it was the last to begin construction. Started in April 1846, the Pennsylvania got through the six separate ranges that make up the Alleghenies in western Pennsylvania in less than seven years. The Philadelphia-to-Pittsburgh route opened for regular service in December 1852.

A group of ten "short-line" railroads that connected Albany and Buffalo was the fourth East-West route to open. By snaking through a series of river valleys (including the Hudson, the Mohawk, and several smaller rivers), the route avoided the heights of the Catskills. The group opened regularly scheduled service in 1853. In the same year, it became the New York Central when it was brought together by Erastus Corning. In the late 1860s, it was purchased by Cornelius Vanderbilt and became the New York Central System. He combined it with his New York and Harlem and Hudson River railroads to complete a single line between New York City and Buffalo.

The last of the other four railroads to reach its western goal was the Baltimore and Ohio. The B&O reached Cumberland, Maryland, at the base of the Alleghenies by November 1842. It was, however, slightly over eleven more years before the route opened for regular traffic between Baltimore and Wheeling, West Virginia, on the Ohio River. Its route to the West was no doubt the hardest, because it included cutting roadbeds from the sides of sheer cliffs as well as drilling long tunnels—11 tunnels and 113 bridges between Cumberland and

Wheeling. By the time it completed the main line to Wheeling, the B&O had spent over $15 million, or three times the expected cost.

Other Developments / There is no doubt that the most important railroading development of the 1840s was the crossing of the various mountain ranges that make up the Appalachians. The second most important development was beginning to connect the North-South coastal short-line railroads. Although a combined system from Florida to Maine would not occur until after the Civil War, each time two short-line railroads met, the system improved.

Another improvement introduced during the 1840s was the telegraph. The telegraph was of great importance because it allowed the railroads to quickly send messages needed to run them. The telegraph's inventor, Samuel F. B. Morse, used the B&O right-of-way between Washington and Baltimore to put up the line that carried the first electrically transmitted message, "What has God wrought?" It was chosen by the daughter of the U.S. commissioner of patents, Ann Ellsworth. The message was sent from the chambers of the Supreme Court Building in Washington and received at the Pratt Street Station in Baltimore on May 24, 1843.

In September 1850, Congress began giving fed-

*Progress in the nineteenth century in
America was marked by the appearance and
invention of the steam press, the telegraph,
the locomotive, and the steamboat.*

eral land to the states to give to the railroad companies. These first "land grants" went to Illinois, Mississippi, and Alabama so that a North-South railroad could be built through these three states and two others, Kentucky and Tennessee.

In Europe and in much of the rest of the world, governmental support and control of railroads led almost immediately to *nationalized railways*. Railroads in the United States, however, were left to private business. Those states that did try to build state-owned railways, among them Illinois, Michigan, and Georgia, failed miserably and lost huge amounts of money.

From the beginning, railroad builders, unable to obtain enough money, tried to get government money to build their new railroads. Until the first land-grant law, the federal government helped the railways by providing special legislation lowering the *tariff duties*, and necessary engineering skills. The reduced tariffs lowered the cost of iron to be used in railroad construction. The engineering skills were provided by military engineers, who surveyed routes, decided which route would be the best for construction, and then laid out the measurements for the construction crews to follow. State and local governments also often provided large amounts of needed money.

The land-grant law to help build a North-South railroad also set the stage for the next decade of railway development (1851–1860). This line was to start at LaSalle, Illinois, on the Illinois and Michigan Canal and end at Mobile, Alabama, on the Gulf of Mexico. At the northern end, two branch lines would be built, going to two small Illinois towns. To the west, the branch would run to a small Mississippi River port, Dunleith (now known as East Dubuque). To the east, the branch would run to a small lake port at the southern tip of Lake Michigan, Chicago. This is probably the last time any railroad route running to Chicago, which was to become known as the "Hub" of the nation's railroad system, would be viewed as merely a branch line.

5 OPENING THE MISSISSIPPI VALLEY

The opening of the great Mississippi-Missouri-Ohio river basin was tied in many ways to the growth of Chicago. In the 1830s, Chicago was a small lake village of three hundred settlers and the basin was a sparsely settled region with few roads for commerce outside its river towns and villages. Illinois, like Michigan and Indiana, experimented with state-owned-and-constructed railroads during the late 1830s and early 1840s and failed. By the end of the 1840s, Illinois found itself, like its sister states, on the edge of financial disaster. These states, while rich in land, had no way to meet the transportation demands of the millions of new immigrants settling there.

In September 1850, the federal government was as short of cash as these states, but it did own a billion and a half acres of land. So it came to the aid of Illinois (and Mississippi and Alabama) in the only way it could, with the first land-grant law. The federal government gave title to the states to a large number of acres of land next to the proposed route of the new railroad through the states. The states were then allowed to give a part of what they received to private railroad companies, which would build the needed railroads on some of the land. The railroad companies also used the land given to them as *collateral* to raise money from private investors. Everyone profited. Most importantly, needed transportation was provided.

In the case of the Illinois Central Railroad, the grant was for 2,595,133 acres. As the building of the railroad began, this land along the right-of-way increased tremendously in value. Land that had not been worth even $1 an acre before September 1850 was now being bought by new settlers and land speculators for from $5 to $25 an acre.

The Illinois Central completed what was at that time the longest railroad in the world just three days before the required date (September 21, 1856). Even though the land grants helped, privately invested money was mainly responsible for building the nation's railroads.

Although the Illinois Central was at first larger and more important, the Galena and Chicago Union Railroad (later the Chicago and Northwestern Railroad) was the first railroad into Chicago (1848) and

THE ILLINOIS CENTRAL RAILROAD CO.

OFFER FOR SALE

1,000,000 Acres of Superior Farming Lands,

IN FARMS OF

40, 80 & 160 Acres & Upwards at from $8 to $12 per acre.

THESE LANDS ARE

NOT SURPASSED BY ANY IN THE WORLD,

THEY LIE ALONG THE

WHOLE LINE OF THE ILLINOIS CENTRAL RAILROAD.

FOR SALE ON

Long Credit, Short Credit or for Cash.

THEY ARE SITUATED NEAR

TOWNS, VILLAGES, SCHOOLS AND CHURCHES.

FOR ALL PURPOSES OF AGRICULTURE, | GRAIN AND STOCK RAISING.

An Illinois Railroad Company
land-offering advertisement

[50]

provided the city with the incentive to grow. The railroad helped the grain elevators expand their business 900 percent in just one harvest. When Chicago's businessmen realized this, an ordinance (a local law just for that city) forbidding the building of a train depot in the town quickly disappeared. Twelve years later, in 1860, there were eleven separate railroads meeting in Chicago, and the "Railroad Hub" of America was born.

The Pioneer, *the first locomotive in Chicago*

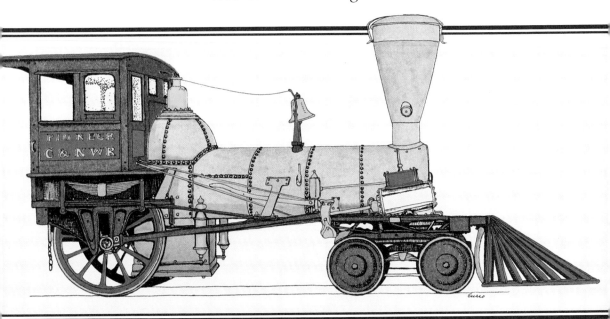

Connecting the Wilderness / The large numbers of immigrants during the 1840s and 1850s supported more railroads.

As the new lines were built, the need to survive meant that each line needed to keep shipping costs low to encourage business. Each railroad also needed to bring in freight customers and passengers from as large an area as possible. Branch lines, called "spur lines," were tried, but they were often too expensive to maintain for the actual profit they provided.

Again the plank roads used earlier in Canada and New York came into play. In the Northern states (Michigan, Wisconsin, Illinois, and Indiana), these roads served as inexpensive "feeder" lines. They helped to move produce and freight to and from the main lines. In the South, plank roads were more often in direct competition with the railroads. The success of plank roads in the South seems to have slowed the area's business growth.

The Four Move West / Four of the five railroads that crossed the Appalachians continued west toward Chicago and the Mississippi River. The Baltimore and Ohio eventually reached both St. Louis and Chicago. It connected with other roads where possible and built on its own when necessary. The

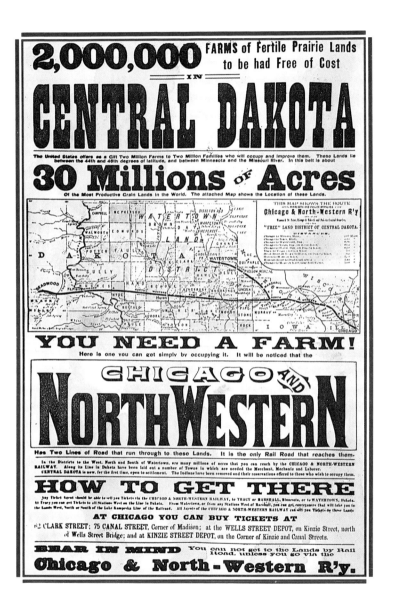

*A Chicago & North-Western poster promoting
free homestead land in the Dakota territory*

Pennsylvania Railroad also reached both St. Louis and Chicago by consolidating with or leasing the tracks of other lines. The New York Central arrived at Chicago by connecting with the Michigan Central and the Michigan Southern. Only the Erie failed to reach Chicago, getting only as far west as Dayton, Ohio. The Erie was held back by both poor management and very broad-gauge track. It used a 6-foot-wide (1.8 m) track. Its locomotives and cars could not travel on the narrower-gauge track used by other railroads.

The South / The South was to end the 1850s with only half the track mileage of the North. Despite a series of financial problems that could have brought construction to a standstill, the Southern railroads connected the southeastern Atlantic coast with the Mississippi River. These financial problems would have ended the South's effort if it had not been for the major support of English investors and aid from the federal government. The South may well have recovered and gone on to prosperity if the Civil War had not occurred when it did.

Lincoln and the Railroads / Abraham Lincoln first gained national prominence as a successful trial lawyer representing railroads. Lincoln worked for both the Illinois Central and the Chicago and Rock Island railroads. His most famous cases were for the Chicago and Rock Island against the steamboat companies. The dispute was over the first bridge to be built across the Mississippi between Rock Island, Illinois, and Davenport, Iowa.

During this dispute, Lincoln twice went to the Supreme Court of the United States, winning his case both times. These railroad cases gave rise to one of the stories that is part of the Lincoln legend. Supposedly, Lincoln sent the railroad a bill for $2,000 for his services. Considering the fee too high, the railroad's superintendent, an ex-army officer, told Lincoln, "Why, sir, this is as much as Daniel Webster himself would have charged. We cannot allow such a claim." Lincoln's response was to take back the bill, raise the fee to $5,000, and send it back. When it was not paid, he sued in court and collected. That railroad superintendent's name was George B. McClellan, and he later served as one of Lincoln's principal generals during the Civil War.

Equipment Changes / There were many changes in railroad equipment during this period. Most of the changes were of more interest to the mechanical engineer than to the public in need of more transportation. There were, however, two important exceptions. The first involved making all track construction the same (with all railroads using the T rail and the crosstie, and a track width of 4 feet 8 inches, or 1.44 m). This allowed quicker growth of more convenient passenger and freight service. The second exception, the "sleeper car," was certainly the one most noticed by the traveling public.

Sleeper cars first appeared in the early 1830s. They were a poor attempt to compete with the much better accommodations provided by the river steamboats. At first, such cars had three shelves along each side of the car, with "bunks" created by vertical partitions every 5 to 6 feet (1.5 to 1.8 m). Passengers slept fully clothed, except for their boots, since there were no curtains for privacy. There were two blankets provided, but a passenger who wanted a pillow had to use a suitcase.

George M. Pullman had an idea for a more comfortable kind of sleeper car. Pullman's first cars had ten sections with two bunks each (with mattresses, linen, and privacy), two washrooms, and a linen closet, all in a car 48 feet (14.6 m) long with only 6 feet (1.8 m) of head room. The Chicago and Alton Railroad provided Pullman with the cars, and it cost Pullman $2,000 to convert them to sleepers.

Making up the berths in a Pullman sleeper

On the Eve of Civil War / The opening of the great Mississippi-Missouri-Ohio river basin has never captured the imagination of our nation in the same way that the opening of the transcontinental route (the route connecting Omaha, Nebraska, and the West Coast) did. However, the great basin's opening was probably more important, for it provided the broad base necessary for all that was to follow. Track mileage increased during this period from 9,021 to 30,635 (14,518 to 49,302 km), over 240 percent. By the close of the 1850s, America's West was open to the industry and population of the New England and Middle Atlantic states. It was open, too, to the flood of immigrants looking for land and opportunity.

The extension of rails across the great basin drew the Northeastern, Middle Atlantic, and Midwestern states together economically, but separated the Southern states even further. This increasing separation, combined with the strong differences over states' rights and slavery issues, would soon explode into civil war.

The decade's growth in track mileage set an overwhelming transportation base for the North on the eve of the Civil War. The North's lead of 2 miles (3.2 km) of track for every 1 mile (1.6 km) in the South was as important to the war's outcome as all

Railroads had made great advances in comfort and equipment by the late nineteenth century.

Left: *dining at twenty miles an hour west of Chicago in a Pullman hotel car of the transcontinental railroad.*

Below: *interior of a Baltimore and Ohio passenger car.*

of the battles that were fought. The developments in railroading during the 1850s and the early 1860s provided a wide base for future growth. The growth would quickly follow throughout the western half of the nation for the rest of the century and would complete the opening of America's West.

GLOSSARY

Amphibious craft: one that can move on both land and water

Charter: the legal paper that allowed a company to start a railroad

Clipper ships: very fast sailing ships

Collateral: property used as security for the repayment of a loan

Horsepower: a measure of the ability to perform work

Nationalized railways: railroads owned only by the government

Rack-rail track: a rail with teeth on its surface into which a similarly toothed wheel on the locomotive fits, so that when the wheel turned, the locomotive moved

Right-of-way: the narrow strip of land on which the railroad tracks are laid

Roadbed: the foundation of a railroad

Sills: blocks of stone laid in two parallel lines in the roadbed to support the rails

Steam dredge: machine used to clear river and harbor channels by taking sand or dirt from the bottom

Tariff duties: a form of tax placed on goods imported from other countries

INDEX